Verses Penned While Down From the Stars:

Poetry by Stella Muse, Virginia, "Blackbird" (PAW), and C.E. Whitehead

(Arranged and edited by CE Whitehead; biographical notes by R. E. Whitehead, "Blackbird", and CE Whitehead.)

Copyright Tallahassee, Florida, 2016

(For the grandchildren/great grandchildren; also for Sandal)

*If you think that she'll be late
it's just one more Orion date.*

-- Virginia F. Whitehead's Smith College classmates, 1940s

Acknowledgements

Acknowledgements go to: *BlazeVOX 15* for Blackbird's "Crow Tree" and "The Lost"; to *The Cumberland Poetry Review* for C. E. Whitehead's "Atalanta" (1995-6); to *Oyster Boy Review* for C. E. Whitehead's "The Hitchhikers" (1995) and "Preparing for Armageddon (1996); *Pegasus Literary Magazine*, Mount Holyoke College, for C. E. Whitehead's "Leaving the Ballot Box" (Spring, 1977); *Potato Eyes Literary Review* for C. E. Whitehead's "Burning the Japanese Beetles" (1995-6) and "Constellations" (1995-6); *Some Translations from Trobador Poetry, With Introduction and Notes*, unpublished thesis, for C. E. Whitehead's "Anno Domini 1211, Foix" (1980); *Viewpoints*, for Stella Muse Whitehead's "Viewpoints", "Georgia Pines", and "Wind in Autumn" (1963); *Worcester Post* for Virginia F. Whitehead's "Lilac Princess" (1938); *Worcester Telegram* for Virginia F. Whitehead's "Echo" (1939).

Image of Orion Nebula from N.A.S.A., E.S.A., M. Robberto (Space Telescope Science Institute/E.S.A.) and the Hubble Space Telescope Orion Treasury Project Team's Advanced Camera Survey (2004-2005; cdn.spacetelescope.org/archives/images/publicationjpg/heic0601a.jpg)

Stella Muse Whitehead (1890-1979) has been honored by the Poetry Society of Georgia. Her poetry has appeared in many publications in the U.S. and abroad. The Japanese magazine *The Study of Current English* featured her poems with Japanese translations. She was briefly Mississippi's Poet Laureate. In 1963 she published a book of verse, *Viewpoints*. She and son Richard researched the life of early Georgia governor Samuel Elbert. She married Lloyd Howell Cobb Whitehead and raised four children, working as a clerk during the Great Depression.

Anna Virginia Farquhar Whitehead (Virginia F. Whitehead, 1924-2011) as a child came to admire the Danish astronomer Tycho Brahe, and to plan a career in astronomy. She was a scholarship student at Smith College during World War Two, where, despite New England's cloudy conditions, she majored in astronomy, completing extensive observations of, and a thesis on, variable stars. She also served as civil air raid warden. She went on to work as a civilian for the Department of Defense. She then worked at Lick Observatory on Mount Hamilton, in California, where she collected more data on "variable stars" and hiked avidly. From Mount Hamilton, she moved to White Sands, New Mexico, to work for RCA (today Lockheed/United Space Alliance) in the early missile program. There she met her future husband. The couple lived for a while on a sailboat, "The Sea Queen", navigating the Gulf of Mexico, but settled down when children came. She later worked in door-to-door sales, and as a teacher, store clerk, and engineer.

"Blackbird" (PAW, 1956-), the first of four children, grew up beside the Banana River. She adored Yeats and Blake as a child, but the initial influence on her own verse was Poe. Later she was drawn to Plath. Today she enjoys Tolkien. She also loves the nature writing of her grandmother. She is one course shy of a bachelor's degree in art. She has collected data for the phone directory, and has also worked as a babysitter (as a teen), a waitress, a floral arranger, a delivery truck driver, and a store clerk. She has three children.

CE Whitehead (1957-) was a middle child. She too grew up beside the Banana River. She learned Spanish at age six, from classmates and a discarded textbook. Like the other three poets, she began writing poetry in grade school. She did not really study verse forms till college. There she studied various forms, including the sestina which she never quite mastered, in preparation for doing verse translations of troubadour songs. Her senior year in college she abandoned English verse in order to focus on the troubadours. She worked her way through college (her mother helped out senior year) and has since earned a master's degree and worked odd jobs (clerk, fast food worker, teacher, writer, technology assistant, dish washer, security guard, farm worker, call center worker).

Contents

Acknowledgements 4

Biographical

Stella Muse Whitehead 5
Virginia F(arquhar) Whitehead 5
"Blackbird" 5
CE Whitehead 5

Situations in Space-Time

Virginia F. Whitehead: **I Saw Time the Other Night** 8
CE Whitehead: **The Universe** 9
CE Whitehead: **Preparing for Armageddon** 9
"Blackbird": **The Legions of the Night** 10

That Starry Sky

Stella Muse Whitehead: **Viewpoints** 11
Virginia F. Whitehead: **Star Friends** 11
CE Whitehead: **Constellations** 12

The Nature of Earth Below

Stella Muse Whitehead: **Georgia Pines** 13
Virginia F. Whitehead: **A Little Gray Squirrel** 13
Virginia F. Whitehead: **Echo** 13
CE Whitehead: **Enclosures** 14
"Blackbird": **Two Lines on a Garden** 15

Mythical Earth

Virginia F. Whitehead: **Lilac Princess** 16
"Blackbird": **The Lost** 17
"Blackbird": **Lilith** 17

Myths or Legends of Love

CE Whitehead: **Portrait** 19
CE Whitehead: **The Hitchhikers** 20
CE Whitehead: **Atalanta** 20
"Blackbird": **Under the Pale Moon's Waning Light** 21
"Blackbird": **Parasite** 21

Everyday

Virginia F. Whitehead: **I Have Come Down from the Stars for a While**	23
Virginia F. Whitehead: **June 4**	24
CE Whitehead: **Bourbon St.**	24
CE Whitehead: **For Christmas**	25
CE Whitehead: **Leaving the Ballot Box**	25
"Blackbird": **Crow Tree**	26

Seasons, Past and Present

Stella Muse Whitehead: **Wind in Autumn**	27
Virginia F. Whitehead: **Spring of the Year is a Long Time Coming**	27
CE Whitehead: **Anno Domini, 1211, Foix**	28
CE Whitehead: **Burning the Japanese Beetles**	30

I. Situations in Space-Time

I Saw Time the Other Night
by Virginia F. Whitehead

(Inspired by Emily Dickinson perhaps)

I saw time the other night;
It came with slow soft feet
And measured tread above the stars
Where roof and skyline meet.
I saw time the other night --
I did not hear it pass;
But I felt its presence as one
Feels a wind wave in tall grass.

I saw time; I felt it move
And shake the whole wide world,
And set it spinning through the night --
Through space unbounded hurled.
And then I tried to count the stars;
But time got in the way
And down the western hills
It chased the stars away.

I saw time; I felt its power,
Relentless and untamed,
Through space, where hot stars flamed.
I could not stop the driving force.
Unyielding, time came on.
But with the same unswerving course
Earth turned to meet the dawn.

(1943)

The Universe
by CE Whitehead

(On reading George Gamov, *1-2-3, Infinity!*)

The universe:
a word at first
that seems to be
the things I see,

and then it grows
to things I know,
and then is filled
by things I willed.

My imagination
it is instead,
but cannot fit
inside my head.

(*1971/1972*)

Preparing for Armageddon
by CE Whitehead

The city's glow spreads dome-like in the background
where you live like a dog in the hills,
alone, half-crazed,burying things --
coins, canned goods, rifles, yourself.
You move secretly through the darkness,
stowing your goods, hiding in foxholes.
The world may be ending, may have ended,
and the dark be perpetual.

But it is the world you are entrenched in --
from the distance a small globe of light,
among other small globes, against a dark background.
Nearer it is simple and round
and flat at the poles.
Nearer still are the ridges and valleys
and your damned foxhole.

You want to know where the end is.
The night is stony and black.
You want to know where the end is.
You hone your knife-blade.
You consult your map.

(1982, 1983, 1985)

The Legions of the Night
by Blackbird

Egyptian eyes are staring
into space, ages of staring, into time,
like unblinking eyes drawn on a butterfly.
The carnelian kite and lace wing
have taken flight
into the deepest bleakish night.
And when the stars have gone away
butterflies of light will flutter by like phantoms,
neon spirits, dark-winged sprites.

Calling out, they beckon us
to follow them, follow time,
On a path under a blackened sun.
In a place where stars have lost their light.
They say to us, come join us now,
become like us, the legions of the night.

(2014)

II. That Starry Sky

Viewpoints
by Stella Muse Whitehead

Why is it thought a thing insane
To dance with the moon down a lonely lane?
It's quite an enchanting thing to do,
On a night of silver . . . a night of blue.
Perhaps my neighbor with lifted brow
Thinks me a trifle odd somehow,
But it doesn't matter much to me,
As long as the white moon dances with me.

My neighbor's concern is with Mistress Brown
And the things that happen about the town,
But the moon knows the place of fairy rings,
Of rainbow trails and butterfly wings,
And talks to me of love and faith,
And all those things that outlive death.

So why is it thought a thing insane,
To dance with the moon down a lonely lane?

(*1963*)

Star Friends
by Virginia F. Whitehead

Altair, Capella, Vega blue,
Aldebaran, Deneb too.
Rigel, and red Arcturus,
Fomalhout, and Polaris,
Bellatrix, and Betelgeuse,
(the Hunter proud lays claim to these);

Castor, Pollux, Sirius,
Phoscyon, Spica, and Pegasus.
All these stars and many more
Shall be my friends forevermore.

(*before 1941*)

Constellations
by CE Whitehead

(for my students, who inspired this, especially for my beginning astronomy laboratory students)

I'm told that a queen sits rocking, in her jeweled chair,
all night, circling the pole star.
She goes nowhere. I point there,
not finding her.
In the dark's nebulous glare,
what planet, what star, is not blurred
past recognition? Like the hum of crickets
in a near meadow, dark came pre-ordained
and even the moon tonight is eclipsed by trees.

Not the dog star, but a mere dog barks,
until the spinning axis yields
a sky out of this earth, a singing field.

(*1981; revised slightly, 2013*)

III. The Nature of Earth Below

Georgia Pines
by Stella Muse Whitehead

I have loved pine trees . . . the balanced grace
of slender trunks, reaching starward . . .
the green lace in silhouette against the sky;
I have revelled in the fragrance
of pine needles burning in the sun
like incense on some lonely alter . . .
the quiet sound of leaves sighing in the wind
breaking the moonlight, and my heart,
in little pieces:

But to love the pines eternally
one must have lived long years
in the burning desert of city streets,
and one must move suddenly from the parched glare,
into the cool fragrance . . . the sea-green shadows of pines
where slender needles point starward in the night,
or burn like incense in the noonday sun.

(*1963*)

A Little Gray Squirrel
by Virginia F. Whitehead

A little gray squirrel sat in the tree
And he kept scolding and scolding me.

(*1931/1932*)

Echo
by Virginia F. Whitehead

Sweet and clear, far and wild,
Calls the elfin echo child;
Gay and free, mockingly,
Her airy notes float back to me

From the hilltop, by the lake,
From the silent woodland brake.

When I roam, no matter where,
She is always lurking there.

When I call, this merry sprite
Answers me, but hides from sight.
I hear her whistle far ahead,
I hurry on but she has fled.

Oft in vain I would pursue,
In my heart I always knew
A pair of mortal eyes like mine,
A glimpse of her could never find;

Elusive, laughing, fairy thing,
She'd mock a beggar or a king.

(*1939*)

Enclosures
by CE Whitehead

> *. . . Only the simplest of animals perceives the universe as it is*.
>
> -- Donald E. Carr; quoted in Annie Dillard, *Pilgrim at Tinker Creek*

Here, perception, through observation,
is the scientist's art, and knows its bound --
no sky. At least no sky is visible
from the basement, where he peers through
the microscope's window to an amoeba.

He adjusts his focus.
Limned by the lense, the amoeba --
fine specimen -- it splits,

And his wife, unsettled in white sheets,
in a white room across town,
twisting fine hair around a puzzling finger.
She says, *the air is leaving*,
and she wants to keep
algae in the room for oxygen
because the room is small --
she has seen it all.

(Funds are hard to come by,
these days go to splitting atoms.)

The funding they won't give him.
The algae they won't give her,
the simplicity of the amoeba
under distant glass, and the atoms
of an air that leaves -- simple?

What do these see? --
or if they cannot see, imagine? --
unseen by him, or her --
who has imagined them --
the imaginer, the imagined --
each in its enclosure.

(*1978; 1993, 1995; 2002; 2009*)

Two Lines on a Garden
by Blackbird

You have buried your garden
in the desert.

(*2012*)

IV. Mythical Earth

Lilac Princess
by Virginia F. Whitehead

The lilac bush is a princess
 Dressed in a lavender gown;
On the top of her head she wears
 A silver moonbeam crown.

She dances on a carpet of the
 Greened, softest grass.
And gazes up at the heavens
 To see the moon sail past.

I wonder what she is thinking,
 As she dances all the while;
It must be something pleasant
 For she always has a smile.

She has never spoken to me
 But once I heard her sing
Of a night that was silver with moonlight,
 And a magic fairy ring.

Perhaps one evening she wandered
 And stumbled on fairy land,
 And deep in the heart of a forest
 She found a fairy band.

And she gazed on fairy revels,
 No mortal should ever see;
So the fairies waved their magic wands
 And changed her into a tree.

They doomed her to dance in the garden;
 How long we cannot tell,
But until a prince comes riding
 And breaks the magic spell,

Often I'd sit and watch her
 Dance, 'neath the pale moon's light;

She'd look at me and be smiling,
 Perhaps he would come that night.

(*1938*)

The Lost
by Blackbird

So pure they were of heart, the essence of all
that was true.
The innocent ones who dwell no more in the land
that was known as Middle Earth. Plucked out too soon like a child that was
taken at birth, like a child taken at birth.

The Balroy chased them all, all of them
into the western sea.

And now they are just a memory, only a memory.
Some say that they followed a star west to the
realm of Valinor.

But then others will tell you that their legs
fell off while traveling north in the sea.
Guided they claim a light from afar.
They seek out eternity, in search of eternity.

(*2003*)

Lilith
by Blackbird

Upon a mighty horse of white
she commands the legions of the night
a fairy queen of noble birth
claimed back the Grail from those on Earth
with a royal falcon on her hand --
she struck a covenant with man
never to be a mortal bride,
for a scarlet shade rides by her side,
and none can claim her love but one
who waits for her within the deep
with broken dreams and restless sleep
a serpent of old rose from the deep
and put all of Heaven into a dark sleep.

And someday under flaming skies
the great-winged serpent shall once more rise --
regal, she is dressed in gold and white,
an angel named Lilith,
Fairy Queen of the night.

(2005)

V. Myths or Legends of Love

Portrait
by CE Whitehead

(for my mother, thinking of a photo taken of her in New Orleans, at the "Cafe of the Two Sisters", with a gentleman)

Sitting
in a corner of a room, looking at
a faded snapshot
in an album of old photographs --
her silhouette, bent
and a little worn
like her picture:
   in it she
   is sitting in a restaurant, her face
   crisp and smooth, no line, no trace, no aging domesticity
   yet etched in.

Now
she sits, late night
in a corner rocker
reading
last week's headlines.

Where are the newer photographs?
She lays down the paper,
stares out the windows.
The moon staring back at her,
stares in.

Mother, where are you now?
You? Yourself in me?
Yourself as you were, looking at that photo,
wrapped in a worn-out sweater,
holding coffee,
wrapped by a future
on which we never could agree.

(*31 March, 1976; revised slightly 2012, 2014*)

Notes
Mom had traveled to New Orleans to visit her sister -- then a nurse at Charity Hospital.

The Hitchhikers
by CE Whitehead

> *For the gods do take all sorts of transformations,*
> *appearing as strangers from elsewhere*
> -- Homer, *The Odyssey*

Their presences drop back as haze,
into no early light. Rounding the devil's own blind bend
the road's winding settles into us,
and we forget those other possibilities
lining the highway and the way back

As if they could stop the wheels' dry spin,
the weave of asphalt. We drive on
with nothing to follow then
beyond a strobic beam, and the engine's echo
curling through the canyon.

Vermillion sinks into black behind us.
Ahead the distances unfurling,
then narrowing. And we are hurtling
into them, or do they compact against us? We are spiraling
into that point.

(*1978*)

Notes
C. E. had hitched to a job as a waitress in Oregon in the summer of 1976 -- she did take a bus briefly for the finale from north of Sacramento when a truck she had caught a ride on had brake problems. That was probably C. E.'s most adventurous hitchhiking trek -- except for hitching winter around Montreal and Quebec when in college and hitching as a teen to University of Southern California ending up in a car driven by runaway teens -- what a disaster – the car was their grandpa's; they would not turn homewards; she left them finally, dismayed, and went to visit a friend of her Mom's; she also hitched some in Europe but mostly used bikes and trains.

Atalanta
by CE Whitehead

The apples were gold
when they spun, gold
rolling past me.
And the boy tossing them --
he too was beautiful,
moving, and fluid.

But when I stooped to catch the third fruit
a worm stuck its head
through the plain, brown skin.
That evening I was wed.

Rot has since eaten the apples,
and my husband's hands are clumsy and cold --
no longer the hands of that boy in the wind.

Gold is mere motion --
and if I could do it again,
I'd kick the apples and keep running!

(*1981*)

Under the Pale Moon's Waning Light
by Blackbird

Ravisher, did you not know I only
came to dance with you
under the full moon's silver light?
You took of me when I was she, the
swan, so I was gone.
I found a helper in the desert, a
harvester of souls.
I gave to him some amber and he
gave to me your soul.
And now it's mine forever to have,
to keep, to hold.

And by the way, we danced that day,
or should I say that night, under the
pale moon's waning light, under the
pale moon's waning light.

(*2003*)

Parasite
by Blackbird

Crucified on a flaming cross, my eyes blaze with
green fire.
But still in your hunger you draw me near,
Beast of blood I
pulse wild with rage.

Must you always wound what you can't love?
Parasite, you still infect me.
Foul poisons fill my soul, snuffing out its radiance.
Like a moth to a flame, you gravitate to me.
But only to ravage and desecrate.
With the oily skin of some slimy slithering thing.
You squirm and beg for your way in,
sucking at my veins, again and again,
like the blood sucking leach you are,
invading a holy shrine.
Get out of my skin, you leper.
I am too pure for you, for anyone!
Hiss away viper!
I shall drink no more of your bitter wine.
Taste no more of the pomegranate's foul red
fruits, while chained to you in the night.
Chained by a feeble bond of blood.
You despicable worm,
You rotten thug.
Must you always kill what you can't love?

(1988)

VI. Everyday

I Have Come Down from the Stars for a While
by Virginia F. Whitehead

I have come down from the stars for a while
To live upon earth again;
I have come down from the stars for a while
To live in the world of men.
People are all about me now;
I, too, am part of the throng;
We've worked together and played together --
I, too, now belong.

Have you not heard the song we sing --
A vibrant stirring song
Of the hum of wheels and the clash of steel?
Wordless, the workman's song.
Have you not felt it as we worked?
That rhythm soars and sings
Up from the shafts and shining rods,
From the gears and piston rings.

We have been working side by side
Under the summer sun;
Our muscles ache and our backs are sore,
But we laugh when the day's work is done.
We still remember how to dream --
Our dreams can never die;
Our hearts shall always feel
The beauty of a starry sky.

I have come down from the stars for a while
To live on the earth below;
I have come down away from the stars --
I think they are closer now.

(*1944*)

Notes
Virginia may have written this after her summer spent picking apples -- during her college days.

June 4
by Virginia F. Whitehead

No poem!

There's always a poem
When the heart has wings
Buried somewhere perhaps
So as not to intrude on
Your business world.
Or only half-written
the rest filed mentally between:

Don't forget cat's eyedrops
+ call the plumber in the morning.

But there's always a poem.
The heart could not stop if it willed.

(*1960s*)

Bourbon St.
by CE Whitehead

(New Orleans, Louisiana)

Small children dance
on Bourbon St.
They shake their hips
and stomp their feet
To the tune of the wrinkled man
who plays harmonica
and grins.

On Bourbon St.
small children dance!
With shining coins
stoning them
swiftly does
the crowd move in.

(*Spring, 1974*)

For Christmas
by CE Whitehead

The grass:
entangled
in your silver chain-linked fences;
love's fresh lemon scent,
now in a chrome-capped bottle;
beauty, sprayed
from a push-button can.

If you can, if you can
giftwrap, glittertrap
your latest smile
for Christmas.

(1974)

Leaving the Ballot Box
by CE Whitehead

> *I pull the curtain back,*
> *and something has gone wrong*
> -- Laura Jensen, "After I Have Voted"

When you pull the curtains back,
it's an old light that greets you,
with its new strangeness --
it's not the light of the black box
from which you have emerged
to these strangers, who tabulate your right to.

You submerge again, this time
behind the *Daily News*, and its cries --
rises, lulls of Dow Jones stocks,
and what looks like an ancient battle,
but newly framed, and far away
in the A.P. Photo.

But it's only sunlight glancing off you
as you make it through an exit.

You glance down at your watch,
as if looking into time.
Buzzards revolve like clockwork
in the mind.

(*Spring, 1977*; revised 1990)

Crow Tree
by Blackbird

It is time you came back home Old Sam,
come on home to crow tree,
where the crows are thick,
like overripe melons on the vine.
And sink your feet in the quicksand
of honeysuckle and southern pine.
I thought I would make it in this world,
I thought I would do just fine,
but little birds can never fly
when their wings are wrapped with twine.
Alone I sit inside my house.
I rock both night and day.
I stare at the walls, and at the ceiling too.
There is no other way.
And I sit atop the highest branch
in that weather-beaten tree,
and caw at the moon,
when the sky grows dark
while Old Sam answers me.
So come back home to crow tree
to the hoodoos that are there.
They will bind your legs and your hands to it,
and no one ever cares.

(*2014*)

VII. Seasons, Past and Present

Wind in Autumn
by Stella Muse Whitehead

Wind in autumn weather
Whimpering 'till dawn,
Searching for the roses
Now that they have gone.

Whirl your dusty questionings
Up into the eaves,
The only answer you will get
Is little crisping leaves.

Sweep with ghostly footsteps
Down the garden stair,
Never a rose will answer
Never a rose will hear.

Wind in autumn weather
Whimpering 'till dawn,
Never search for roses
Once they have gone.

(*1963*)

Spring of the Year is a Long Time Coming
by Virginia F. Whitehead

Spring of the year is a long time coming,
Poor mother nature,
poor little robins,
poor little butterfly
waiting for their spring.
Spring for my heart,
Maverick thing,

Anytime in summer,
Anytime in autumn,
Anytime in winter,
Anytime in spring,
Any night at seven,

When your footsteps bring
New life to my winter
My heart has its spring.

(*1960s*)

Anno Domini, 1211, Foix
by CE Whitehead

It was a choked spring. De Montfort
got up both drums and peace offers.
His words puffed like wind off the Garonne.
We turned plows over for arms.
Our count Raymond Roger would stand no truce.
So we passed
   silenced bells, bared altars, locked churches.

The priests too marched through the town gates,
carrying out the Eucharist on platters,
ritual backs turned on their villages.

April we rode out to the wood of Montgey,
lay in ambush, descended
on a handful --
scullions, Germans
enroute to Simon's camp --
and smote them.

This in a few days. Then news from Lavaur
of retaliation, burnings, a woman
stoned to death at a well's bottom.

That summer the campaign progressed,
laid waste to the Roman road
and we smote our own fields.
They seized Castelnaudry. In September
we fell like locusts upon that city,
Overtook on the highway
Simon's hirelings,

Full force they charged us
and we, blow for blow parrying,
and my companion pared by one of them
and I know Death's hand
And the devil take it.
This is no tournament.

But the South before this
was rank with peace
and Raymond of Toulouse
like King Richard -- that old "Yes-and-No" --
wavering on horseback.

Now furrows in the land have opened
wide with blood. De Montfort's crusaders
barricade themselves at Pamiers.

Out here we patrol the dead
in stripped fields.

(*Fall, 1979*)

Notes
This poem is spoken by an imaginary soldier under the Count of Foix. Nearly every incident mentioned in this poem is described in Jonathan Sumption's well-researched *The Albigensian Crusade*. The allusion to Richard Lionheart, calling him "Yes-and-No", is from the twelfth-century troubadour Bertran de Born's verse which called Richard "mon Oc-e-No", 'my Yes-and-No'. Karen Wilkes Klein's *The Partisan Voice* discusses Bertran de Born in some depth. Bertran de Born, perhaps a bit of a nationalist, apparently found Richard Lionheart to be too "dallying" and enjoyed making fun of him rather than joining in several of Richard's military campaigns. (Bertran opposed Richard in one campaign, siding with Richard's brother.)
This poem was originally composed to introduce C. E.'s translations of the troubadours, the subject of her undergraduate thesis, and was the only poem she composed during the 1979-80 year (that year she resigned midterm from her editorial duties with her college literary magazine, *Pegasus*, because she wanted to devote herself wholly to the troubadours and the Middle Ages and related studies).
Simon de Montfort, also from the region known as the Òc, was probably the main figure behind the Albigensian Crusade. De Montfort had a son he wanted to have married, and whom he could not marry off till after Toulouse was overrun, and there was plunder.
Raymond, Count of Foix, was well-situated in the Pyrenees and a good military commander. Raymond Roger is not to be confused with Raymond VI of Toulouse, a count who harbored heretics, and kin to Raymond Roger by marriage. But both Raymonds were allied. Nor is he to be confused with Raymond Roger Trencaval, viscount of Beziers, who was killed at about this time, after the seige of Beziers. For more on the Count of Foix, see http://www.speedylook.com/Raymond-Roger_de_Foix.html. More Albigensian Crusade history, including an outline of the 1211 campaign, can be found at: http://xenophongroup.com/montjoie/albigens.htm).

Burning the Japanese Beetles
by CE Whitehead

(for KJG)

Lingering in the West
I flick the porchlights on
and carry the can of gas
into the once oriental splendor
of a garden. Roses stoop.
Green flickers on their frayed filaments,
and the spectral moon
grazes the rotting leaves,
the copper wings.

The East is awake
in that moon's solemn face,
ghost-risen and it watches
season's end. Petals fold, the gas
can pulling down and to the earth,
a tidal pull. Small moons
swim there, flare white.

And the lights
in other people's houses,
people I do not know,
flicker and die out --
Ash on the horizon.

The beetles are now a black heap
next to the ragged flowers.
Roses for lovers. Roses
for the dead, the beetles
in their soot-black can,
the air thick with gas,
sullen and still volatile.

(1977, 1978; 1982)

Notes
The summer in college before C.E. went to Europe she did house sitting and lawn mowing; part of her work involved removing Japanese Beetles from rose bushes daily (the roses had long been mostly consumed), placing them in a can, pouring gas over them, and igniting them (there was no other way). She called a friend to complain; the friend said, "do not complain; write". So she did.